TOUGH TIMES
to Be a Kid

A Kid's Life in
ANCIENT
GREECE

by

Hermione Redshaw

BEARPORT
PUBLISHING

Minneapolis, Minnesota

Library of Congress Cataloging-in-Publication Data

Names: Redshaw, Hermione, 1998- author.
Title: A kid's life in ancient Greece / by Hermione Redshaw.
Description: Minneapolis, MN : Bearport Publishing Company, [2024] |
  Series: Tough times to be a kid | Includes bibliographical references
  and index.
Identifiers: LCCN 2023011626 (print) | LCCN 2023011627 (ebook) | ISBN
  9798885099523 (library binding) | ISBN 9798888221266 (paperback) | ISBN
  9798888222720 (ebook)
Subjects: LCSH: Children--Greece--History--To 146 B.C.--Juvenile
  literature. | Children--Greece--Social life and customs--Juvenile
  literature. | Greece--Social conditions--To 146 B.C.--Juvenile
  literature. | Greece--Civilization--To 146 B.C.--Juvenile literature.
Classification: LCC HQ792.G73 R43 2024 (print) | LCC HQ792.G73 (ebook) |
  DDC 305.230938--dc23/eng/20230313
LC record available at https://lccn.loc.gov/2023011626
LC ebook record available at https://lccn.loc.gov/2023011627

For more information, write to Bearport Publishing, 5357 Penn Avenue South, Minneapolis, MN 55419.

CONTENTS

Being a  KID

Being a kid is tough. Math class is hard. Your little sister broke your tablet. And your parents are always telling you to stop eating junk food.

HELP!

What could be worse than homework?

But how hard is it, really? If you think being a kid today is tough, imagine what it was like living as a kid in ancient Greece.

You'd be living in a time when there was no sugar, no electricity, and no privacy when you went to the bathroom. That's tough!

ANCIENT GREECE

Get ready to travel back in time and see what life was like for kids in ancient Greece.

Ancient GREECE

Ancient Greeks lived more than 3,000 years ago, in an area much larger than modern-day Greece. This **civilization** spread across Europe, Egypt, and part of Asia.

Some of the fun things we have today came from ancient Greece. It was where **theaters** and plays started. The Greeks also gave us the Olympics. This event was held to celebrate the god Zeus.

Zeus—god of thunder and king of the gods

Not everything in ancient Greece was fun and games. Theaters didn't have snack bars or even ceilings! Plays were performed outside, and the seats were just benches made of stone.

Only men could compete in the Olympics. And they did so completely naked!

When will they invent running shorts?

SURVIVING
the Time

To live in ancient Greece, you would first have to reach childhood. That was tougher than you might think! Many babies died before their first birthdays. Illnesses that we have cures for today might have killed babies in ancient Greece.

Can you take me to the 21st century?

Even being born was dangerous! Doctors and **midwives** did not have the same medicine or **technology** they have today. Most parents simply prayed to the gods for a safe birth.

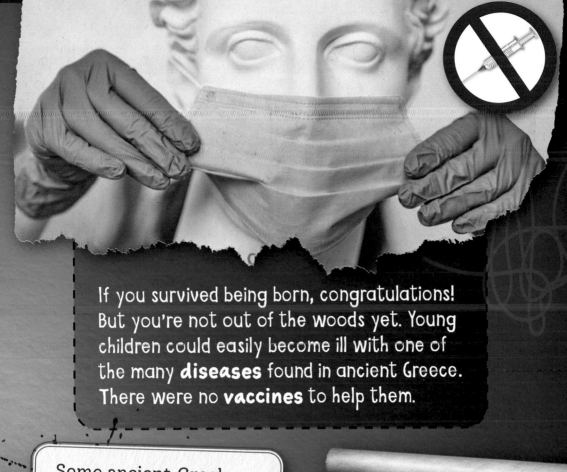

If you survived being born, congratulations! But you're not out of the woods yet. Young children could easily become ill with one of the many **diseases** found in ancient Greece. There were no **vaccines** to help them.

Some ancient Greek cures were as bad as the illnesses themselves. Doctors believed that having too much of certain **fluids** in your body could make you sick. They might drain your blood to make you feel better!

You're not taking my blood!

HEADS
of the Household

At home in ancient Greece, fathers ruled. Dad was the head of the household. Whatever he said, you did.

When I grow up, I'm giving mom the vote.

Your mother would not be allowed to leave the house without your father's permission. Women were not even allowed to vote!

Don't expect to spend time with your dad in ancient Greece. When men weren't working as soldiers, farmers, or **craftsmen**, they would spend time with other men. Those in the army might not see their families for years!

My kids have probably forgotten about me!

Sounds about right.

Me, too.

Same here!

You think you have it tough?

Being a kid is so hard!

Ancient Greek mothers had to take care of the children and the home. They would cook and clean. They also had to make clothes for everyone and collect water.

HOME Muddy Home

What were those homes moms looked after like? In ancient Greece, houses were often made from wood and mud bricks. They didn't have much inside, including furniture.

When it got dark out, most ancient Greeks went to bed. There was no electricity back then, so any light at night had to come from candles or oil lamps. The inside of the home might be just as dark during the day. Windows were often **shuttered** to keep out the hot sun.

I wish my home wasn't so dark and muddy.

Think a dark home would make for a good night's sleep? Forget it! Most families all slept in the same room at night. You might find yourself squashed in a bed with your brothers, sisters, parents, and grandparents!

Homes did not have running water, let alone a shower! People went to public baths to wash or used a bucket or stream. Ancient Greek toilets were public, too! Using the toilet was a **social** event. Everyone sat side by side and chatted—while they did their business!

Honey, I'M HUNGRY

Ancient Greeks did not eat much meat. It was expensive, so only the rich could afford it. Even then, you wouldn't chow down on a hamburger. The best you could hope for was a plate of rabbit, deer, or wild pig.

Maybe you should consider a plant-based diet.

You might also eat octopus. Yum!

Many meals in ancient Greece had fruits, vegetables, and bread. There was no sugar back then, so honey was used as a sweetener.

Dionysus, god of wine

Wine? No, thank you.

In ancient Greece, water was not always clean. So, what did people drink? Wine, mostly. This beverage was so important that the Greeks even had a god for it! As a kid, you'd probably drink grape juice before it turned to wine.

Ancient Greeks didn't use knives and forks. Everyone ate with their fingers. Mealtimes could get pretty messy!

Don't Mess with THE GODS!

The ancient Greeks believed gods and goddesses created the world and kept it running. The gods also had a say in what happened to you. You did not want to mess with an ancient Greek god!

Don't make Zeus angry! You won't like me when I'm angry!

Have you heard of Sisyphus? The gods made him push a large boulder up a hill over and over again—forever! How about Medusa? The goddess Athena turned her hair into snakes! These stories are from Greek **mythology**.

I'm having a bad hair day.

Yesssss.

If something bad happened to you, it was probably because the gods were unhappy. Think of how bad it is to get in trouble with your parents! It was 10 times worse to be punished by a god!

The gods met to decide how to punish bad people.

They can't sacrifice us if they can't reach us!

To keep the gods on your side, you would need to pray to their **statues**. You would leave presents in their **shrines**. Sometimes, people would **sacrifice** animals to make the gods happy.

GREEK CHIC

In ancient Greece, no one dressed in shirts or pants! Most adults wore only a large rectangle of fabric draped over the body and fastened at the shoulder with a pin. This fashion-forward outfit was called a tunic.

As a kid, you'd wear even less than the adults—just a short piece of cloth tied around the waist. Or you may wear nothing at all, especially if you were playing a sport.

Mom, can you please make me some pants?

My ankles are cold.

Not mine!

Tunics could be made of heavy wool or light linen. They were often very colorful and had fancy patterns. Men's tunics went only to the knees, while women's went down to their feet.

Poor people sometimes made tunics from bed sheets.

Statues often show ancient Greeks with curls. It was the fashion of the day. Greeks with straight hair used beeswax to shape curls and hold them firmly in place!

FUNNY BONES and BLADDER BALLS

Ancient Greek children played with toys, just as kids do today. Many toys were not very different from ours. They had balls, dolls, marbles, and even yo-yos. But what these toys were made of might surprise you—or gross you out!

Would you rather play video games or marbles? Children in ancient Greece didn't have video games. They didn't really have marbles, either! Instead of glass balls, they used small animal bones known as knucklebones.

You call this a toy?!

Those kids want to play ball with me!

Umm... I wouldn't if I were you.

Okay, so forget knucklebone marbles. How about playing with a ball instead? Just know the ball might be a bunch of rags tied together. Or it could be a pig's **bladder** filled with air!

Don't hug your clay dolls too tightly! They might shatter!

Ancient Greek dolls weren't exactly soft and cuddly. They were made from clay, wax, or glass!

Ancient Greek dolls

GETTING Schooled

At age seven, Greek boys began going to school to learn poetry, music, reading, writing, and math. They wrote on wooden tablets covered with soft wax. A stylus was used to carve letters and words into the wax.

Gym class was an important part of a boy's education. Running, jumping, wrestling, and throwing spears got him ready to become a soldier!

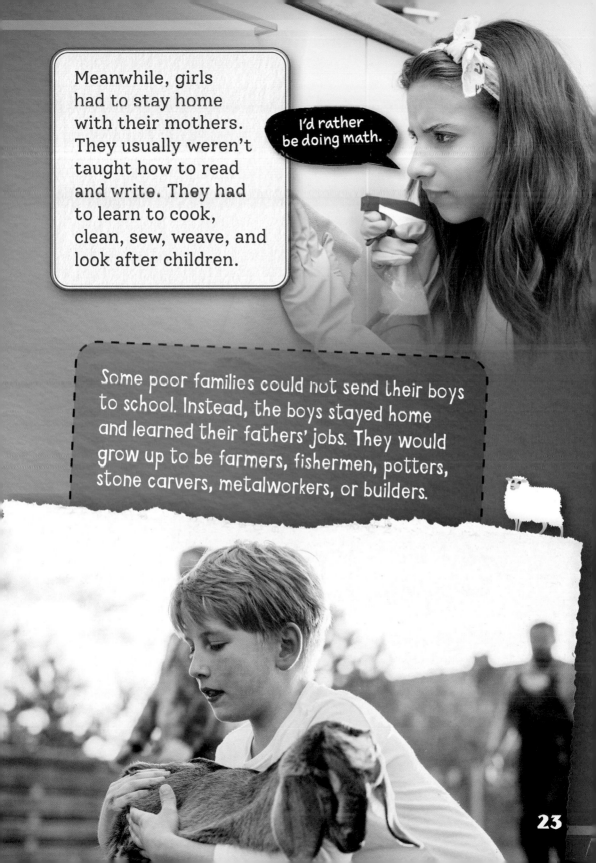

Meanwhile, girls had to stay home with their mothers. They usually weren't taught how to read and write. They had to learn to cook, clean, sew, weave, and look after children.

I'd rather be doing math.

Some poor families could not send their boys to school. Instead, the boys stayed home and learned their fathers' jobs. They would grow up to be farmers, fishermen, potters, stone carvers, metalworkers, or builders.

THE SPARTAN ARMY

Why did my parents move us to Sparta?

Some boys from an area in Greece called Sparta might not go to school at all. Here, children were raised from birth to be soldiers.

Who are you calling weak?!

Even as a baby, you had to be strong in Sparta. Babies who were thought to be weak were sometimes abandoned on a hillside!

We're Spartan! It's the army life for us!

When they were seven, Spartan boys would be taken from their homes to join the army. These kids had to be tough and strong to make it through army training.

Ouch! Ow! I miss my sandals!

The boys would have to march without shoes and go without food. They were forced to fight one another and weren't allowed to complain if they were hurt.

I really miss my mom.

Boys lived away from home because Spartans believed that their mothers would make them weak.

GROWN UP

When?

There were no teens in ancient Greece. Once you were done being a child, you went straight to being treated like an adult. With no one to tell you to clean your room or do your homework, you could do whatever you wanted, right?

Unfortunately, being an adult wasn't so easy. Girls were thought of as adults when they were around 12 years old. They were treated like grownups before boys were. But as soon as they became women, it was time to get married and start a family.

I'M NOT READY TO GET MARRIED!

Marriages in ancient Greece were arranged by a girl's father or other male relative. Girls didn't get to choose their husbands. A bride might not even meet her husband until the wedding day.

Was this the best Dad could find?

Say goodbye to all of your toys once you turn 12. As part of becoming a woman, girls were supposed to give their toys to the gods.

I know you love Mister Snuggles. But the gods want him now!

Boys didn't marry quite as young as girls did, but it was still tough for them. Remember all that early military training? Well, when boys turned 14, they might start putting those skills to use—in the army.

Gym class was way more fun!

What if you didn't want to join the army? Rich boys might be able to keep studying. Ancient Greece had many great **scholars**.

Pythagoras, stop staring at that triangle and mow the lawn!

Pythagoras was a scholar famous for studying triangles.

If you chose to be a farmer, you might still have to join the army. Many ancient Greek farmers were also soldiers. Some of the money they made from farming was used to buy their armor, spears, swords, and shields.

I'd rather be studying triangles.

Greek soldiers had to find their own food. Often, they had dried fish.

If you were poor, don't worry. You might still get to live in a nice house. That is, if you work for rich people. Some servants got to live in big, fancy homes. But they had to do whatever the boss asked of them.

That's TOUGH!

Do you still think being a kid today is tough? At least you don't live in ancient Greece! From crowded mud houses to marching barefoot across battlefields, it was not a fun time to be a kid!

But don't worry. You can relax and return to the present. You don't need to get married to a stranger or join the army. You can go back to enjoying being a kid here and now.

Which part of life in ancient Greece sounds the toughest?

GLOSSARY

bladder a pouch in an animal that holds gas or liquid

civilization a large group of people that shares the same history and way of life

craftsmen people who practice trades, such as carving, metalwork, pottery, or construction

diseases illnesses

fluids liquids that flow and take the shape of their container

midwives women who help other women give birth

mythology the traditional stories of a group used to explain the world and how it was formed

sacrifice to offer something of value to a god or gods in order to please them

scholars people who studied as their main job

shrines places where people pray to gods

shuttered closed with wooden window coverings

social related to a friendly gathering, often with a special purpose or activity

statues models of people or things that are shaped from solid materials

technology the science of making useful things to solve problems

theaters buildings where people go to watch plays and other performances

vaccines types of medicine that protect someone against specific diseases

INDEX

READ MORE

Finan, Catherine C. *Ancient Greece (X-treme Facts: Ancient History).* Minneapolis: Bearport Publishing, 2022.

Reynolds, Donna. *Ancient Greece Revealed (Unearthing Ancient Civilizations).* New York: Cavendish Square Publishing, 2023.

LEARN MORE ONLINE

1. Go to **www.factsurfer.com** or scan the QR code below.
2. Enter "**Tough Times Greece**" into the search box.
3. Click on the cover of this book to see a list of websites.